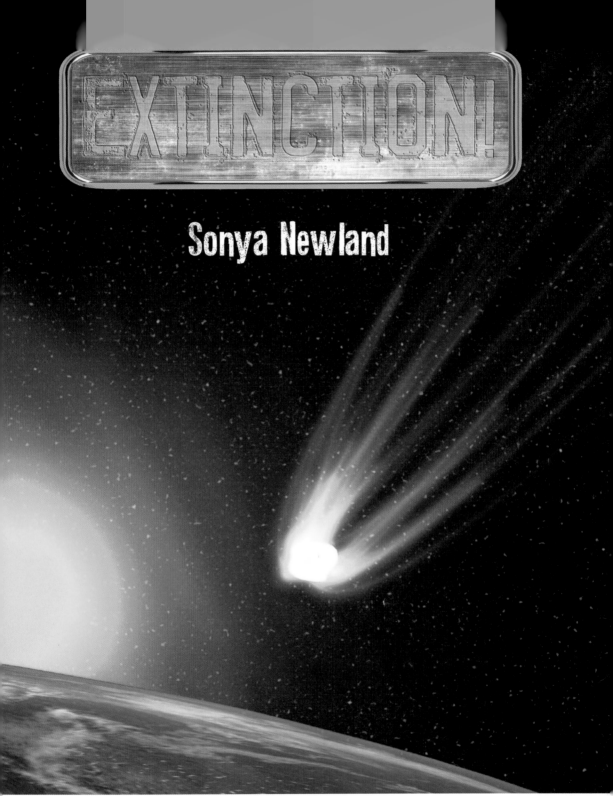

EXTINCTION!

Sonya Newland

Crabtree Publishing Company
www.crabtreebooks.com

Crabtree Publishing Company
www.crabtreebooks.com

Author: Sonya Newland
Publishing plan research and development:
   Sean Charlebois, Reagan Miller
   Crabtree Publishing Company
Photo research: Sonya Newland
Editor: Kathy Middleton
Proofreader: Crystal Sikkens
Design: Tim Mayer (Mayer Media)
Cover design: Margaret Amy Salter
Production coordinator and prepress
   technician: Ken Wright
Print coordinator: Katherine Berti

Produced for Crabtree Publishing by
White-Thomson Publishing

Reading levels determined by
Publishing Solutions Group.
Content level: R
Readability level: L

Photographs:
Alamy: Walter Myers/Stocktrek Images: p. 12;
National Geographic Image Collection: p. 20;
David Lyons: p. 37; G L Archive: p. 41; Corbis:
Mark Garlick/Science Photo Library: pp. 3, 4–5,
26–27; Tui De Roy/Minden Pictures: p. 7; Walter
Myers/Stocktrek Images: pp. 11, 34–35; Ken
Lucas/Visuals Unlimited: p. 13; Robert
Giusti/National Geographic Society: pp. 18–19;
Louie Psihoyos: pp. 21, 30; John Carnemolla:
p. 40; Michael & Patricia Fogden: p. 42; Ralph
Lee Hopkins/National Geographic Society:
pp. 44–45; Dreamstime: Andre Adams: pp. 22–23;
Neverhood: pp. 24–25; Martinzak: p. 35;
Getty Images: pp. 8–9; AFP: p. 43; NASA: JPL-
Caltech/STScI/CXC/SAO: p. 19; Shutterstock:
front cover; Hunor Focze: pp. 1, 28–29; Russell
Shively: p. 8; Vlad61: pp. 10–11; Leonello Calvetti:
pp. 14–15; Andreas Meyer: p. 15; Catmando: pp.
16–17, 38–39; Michael Rosskothen: back cover, p.
16; Steffen Foerster Photography: p. 31;
TJUKTJUK: pp. 36–37; Thinkstock: front cover;
Wikipedia: Ernest Orlando Lawrence Berkeley
National Laboratory: p. 32; Babaudus/Creative
Commons License: p. 33.

Library and Archives Canada Cataloguing in Publication

Newland, Sonya
      Extinction! / Sonya Newland.

(Crabtree chrome)
Includes index.
Issued also in electronic formats.
ISBN 978-0-7787-7925-4 (bound).--ISBN 978-0-7787-7934-6
(pbk.)

      1. Extinction (Biology)--Juvenile literature. I. Title.
II. Series: Crabtree chrome

QH78.N49 2012   j576.8'4   C2012-905533-6

Library of Congress Cataloging-in-Publication Data

CIP available at Library of Congress

Crabtree Publishing Company
www.crabtreebooks.com   1-800-387-7650

Printed in the U.S.A./112012/FA20121012

Published in Canada
Crabtree Publishing
616 Welland Ave.
St. Catharines, ON
L2M 5V6

Published in the United States
Crabtree Publishing
PMB 59051
350 Fifth Avenue, 59th Floor
New York, New York 10118

Published in the United Kingdom
Crabtree Publishing
Maritime House
Basin Road North, Hove
BN41 1WR

Published in Australia
Crabtree Publishing
3 Charles Street
Coburg North
VIC 3058

Contents

Mass Extinctions

The Cycle of Life

About 98 percent of all species that have ever lived on Earth are now extinct, or have died out completely. Most species survive for about ten million years. Perhaps extinction is part of Earth's natural cycle. But when animals become extinct it affects us all and the world we live in.

▼ *The Sun will eventually become what is known as a **red giant**, before dying in a huge explosion.*

What Does the Future Hold?

Could something wipe out all life on Earth today? Could animals and humans be killed by an asteroid crashing into Earth? Could an erupting supervolcano or a deadly virus kill every living thing? Or will we end all life on Earth ourselves by exploding a nuclear bomb that would block out the Sun?

Scientists believe that all life on Earth will probably end in about five billion years. This is when the Sun will die. Without the Sun, nothing can live.

red giant: a star that has grown much larger in size

Life and Death

The first animals appeared on Earth about 600 million years ago (mya). Since then, millions of types of animals have become extinct. Some died out naturally over many years. Others were hunted to extinction by humans. More have died recently because of **climate change**.

600 mya	First animals emerge in the seas
450 mya	Ordovician mass extinction
370 mya	Devonian mass extinction
250 mya	Permian mass extinction
230 mya	First dinosaurs appear
200 mya	First mammals appear
65 mya	Extinction of the dinosaurs
70,000 ya	Humans nearly wiped out by volcano
10,000 ya	Woolly mammoths die out
1662	Dodo becomes extinct
1883	Quaggas die out
1896	Last passenger pigeons shot
1936	Tasmanian tiger becomes extinct
2011	Western black rhinoceros becomes extinct
2012	Last known Pinta Island tortoise dies

▶ *The last Pinta Island giant tortoise, called Lonesome George, died in 2012.*

Big Extinctions

Sometimes, many animals on Earth disappear at about the same time. This is what happened when the dinosaurs died out. The dinosaurs are not the only example, though. There have been at least five of these mass extinctions throughout Earth's lifetime.

Extinction is still happening today, faster than at any time in Earth's long history. Human activities play a big part in this quicker pace.

climate change: changes in the weather over a long time

Shifting Land

The first mass extinction happened about 450 million years ago. It is known as the Ordovician mass extinction. At this time, there was just one continent on Earth. It slowly formed a huge area of frozen land.

▼ *Most animals lived in shallow seas 450 million years ago.*

▲ *This is a fossil of a small sea animal called a trilobite. All trilobites are now extinct.*

Frozen Planet

Most animals lived in the sea. They died out as
seawater turned to ice. There were only a few
land animals. They could not survive the freezing
temperatures of this cold new land. They died too.
Two out of every three **species** became extinct.

Scientists call a mass extinction
an "extinction event." The term
means that something dramatic
happened to kill thousands
of species at the same time.

species: a particular type of animal or plant

Life Returns

Slowly, Earth warmed up again. New types of animals emerged on land and in the sea. The time in history called the Devonian period began. Another mass extinction happened during that period, 370 million years ago. Three-quarters of all species died.

▼ *Coral reefs provide food and shelter for millions of animals that live in the oceans.*

Death in the Sea

Scientists cannot connect the extinction with a single cause, but they know it affected sea animals the most. Even though they live in water, sea animals still need oxygen to breathe. But changes to Earth's climate meant there was not enough oxygen in the ocean any more. Only **bacteria** could survive there.

▲ *Four-legged creatures had just started to live on land when this mass extinction occurred.*

Coral reefs were home to many sea creatures. The reefs were destroyed in the Devonian mass extinction. New ones did not grow for another 100 million years.

bacteria: tiny creatures made of a single cell

Lost World

The worst ever extinction took place about 250 million years ago. This time was known as the **Permian** period. Plants and animals were very different to those around us today. Earth was covered in forests of giant ferns. Lizards the size of rhinos roamed the land.

▼ Dimetrodon *belonged to a group of animals called synapsids that lived in the Permian period.*

The Great Dying

Suddenly, over 90 percent of life on Earth died out. This extinction was so terrible that scientists named it the "Great Dying." It may have been caused by huge volcanoes. When they erupted, they changed Earth's climate.

After the Permian mass extinction, a pig-like animal called *Lystrosaurus* ruled the land. There were almost no other animals left!

▼ *These are fossils of sea scorpions, which died out in the Permian mass extinction.*

 Permian: a period from about 300 to 250 million years ago

Death of the Dinosaurs

The most famous mass extinction is the death of the dinosaurs, 65 million years ago. It was not only the land dinosaurs that died. Flying **reptiles** such as pterosaurs also died. Giant swimming reptiles such as plesiosaurs disappeared from the sea.

Tyrannosaurus rex

▶ *Even great hunters such as the* Tyrannosaurus rex *did not survive this extinction event.*

How on Earth?

The dinosaurs had been very successful at surviving. The time they lived on Earth is called the "Age of Reptiles" because they ruled our planet for 140 million years. Something very dramatic must have happened to make them extinct.

Gallimimus

Modern humans have lived on Earth for a tiny amount of time compared to dinosaurs. We have only been here for about 200,000 years.

▼ *Huge plesiosaurs such as* Elasmosaurus *ruled the oceans during the Age of Reptiles.*

reptiles: cold-blooded animals that lay eggs

The Big Mystery

Searching for the Truth

These mass extinctions happened a very long time ago. It is hard to know what caused them. Scientists spent many years trying to work out what killed the dinosaurs. They came up with a lot of different **theories**.

▲ Microraptor *was a small dinosaur with wings. It was only about the size of a chicken.*

Too Big?

Some dinosaurs were enormous. Perhaps they grew so big that they were crushed by their own weight. But animals do not grow so big that they cannot move! Also, if this idea was true then small dinosaurs would have survived.

The biggest animal ever to live on Earth is still alive. The blue whale weighs a huge 120 tons (108 metric tons). That is much more than any dinosaur.

◀ *Dinosaurs such as* Diplodocus *were huge, but they could still move about quite quickly.*

theories: ideas that have not yet been proven true

17

Flowering Plants

For millions of years, only green plants grew on Earth. Then plants with flowers began to appear. This was near the time that the dinosaurs died. One theory scientists had was that flowers may have been poisonous to the dinosaurs.

▲ *Flowering plants appeared on Earth about 125 million years ago.*

Star Explosion

Another early idea was that an exploding star killed the dinosaurs. When a star dies, it explodes. This is called a supernova. A supernova gives off a burst of **radiation**. Perhaps this radiation reached all the way to Earth, killing the animals.

▲ *A dying star releases radiation that can travel through space. Could this be what killed the dinosaurs?*

 The idea that flowers destroyed life on Earth does not make sense. Many sea animals died, and so did lots of plants!

 radiation: energy that can be harmful to living things

Egg Thieves

Dinosaurs had been around for 30 million years before **mammals** appeared. The mammals were very small. How could they be a threat to the giant dinosaurs? Some people think that mammals ate all the dinosaur eggs. No eggs, no new dinosaurs. They could never have eaten them all, though!

▼ *Bones of an* Oviraptor *were found lying on the nest of another dinosaur.*

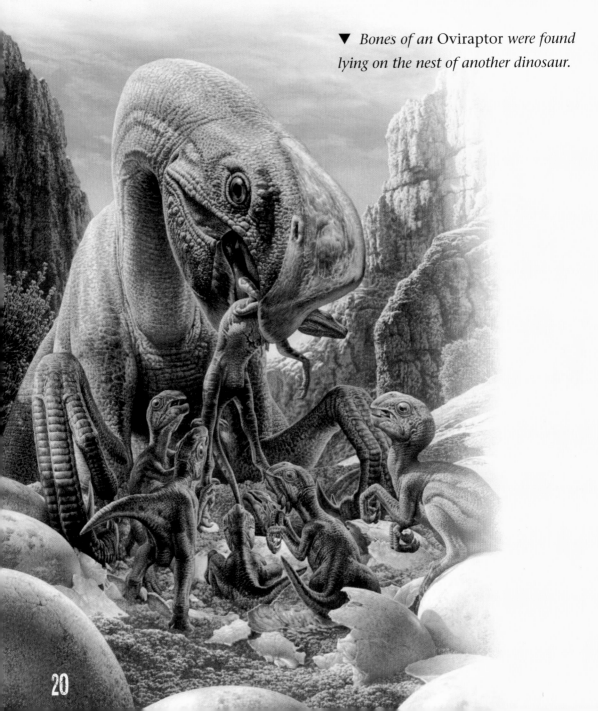

Diseased Insects

Another idea is that tiny bugs killed the dinosaurs.
Some insects spread disease today. Perhaps biting
flies made the dinosaurs ill. But scientists can tell
from bones if dinosaurs had a disease. Not very
many of them did.

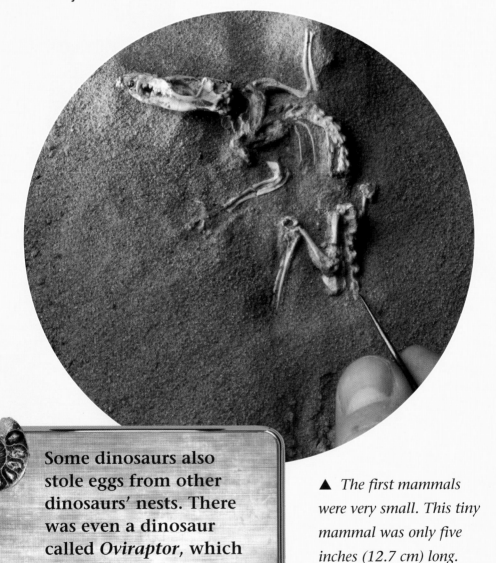

Some dinosaurs also
stole eggs from other
dinosaurs' nests. There
was even a dinosaur
called *Oviraptor*, which
means "egg stealer."

▲ *The first mammals
were very small. This tiny
mammal was only five
inches (12.7 cm) long.*

mammals: warm-blooded animals that give birth to live young

Death by Volcano

Other theories about what killed the dinosaurs seem more likely. There was a huge range of volcanoes in India at the time of the dinosaurs. If some of them erupted together, it would have been a disaster for the planet's animals.

A Killer Cloud

Erupting volcanoes would have pumped
out smoke and dust. This could have
poisoned the dinosaurs. It might also
have changed the weather on Earth.
Living things might not have been
able to **adapt**.

When the dinosaurs died,
the sea was over 1,000 feet
(300 meters) higher than
it is today. Changes in
the weather could have
caused huge floods.

▲ *Volcanoes may have released
enough ash to block out the Sun.
Ash is tiny pieces of rock.*

adapt: to develop different features to survive in new conditions

Killer Asteroid

The Mystery Solved?

From the beginning, most scientists agreed that Earth changed just before the dinosaurs died. They just could not agree why it happened. They also disagreed about how long the change took. Then, in 1980, a scientist called Luis Alvarez had a new idea.

▲ *The asteroid would have brought death to living things all over the world.*

Death from Space

Alvarez found evidence that an **asteroid** had smashed into Earth. The asteroid would have set forests on fire all over the world. It would have caused waves in the sea that were thousands of feet high. It would have sent up a huge cloud of dust, blocking out the Sun for months or maybe even years.

Earth might have been hit by a comet not an asteroid. Comets are giant lumps of ice and rock in space.

asteroid: a lump of rock and metal that moves around in space

Effects of the Asteroid

Some animals would have been killed right away when the asteroid hit. Others would have died when their forest homes caught fire. With no sunlight, the planet would have become very, very cold. Dinosaurs were used to a warm, sunny Earth.

▲ *Over time, Earth turned into a wasteland with very little life.*

Food Chains

Plants cannot survive without sunlight. This means there would not have been enough food for plant-eating animals. As they died, the meat-eating dinosaurs that fed on the plant-eaters would have starved, too.

The asteroid also released chemicals. These poisoned the water on Earth and caused **acid rain**.

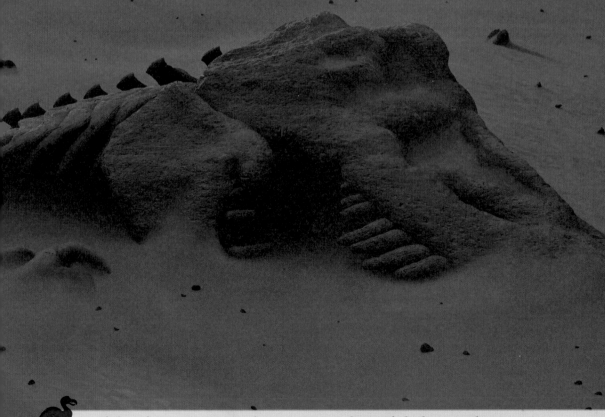

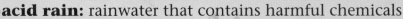

acid rain: rainwater that contains harmful chemicals

Big Impact

The asteroid may have been more than six miles (9.6 km) wide. When it crashed into Earth it was traveling at over 60,000 miles (96,560 km) per second. Such a huge impact would have left a **crater** 100 miles (160 km) wide!

▼ *The asteroid crashed into Earth so hard and so fast that it left an enormous crater.*

The Search for the Crater

No one knew yet where the asteroid might have struck. So the search began. Scientists all over the world began looking for a crater that was the right size. In the late 1980s, hidden under some younger rocks, the Chicxulub crater was found. It measures 112 miles (180 km) wide and 3,000 feet (914 meters) deep.

▲ *The Chicxulub crater lies at the edge of the Yucatan Peninsula in Mexico.*

The craters on the Moon were caused by many asteroids smashing into it over millions of years.

crater: a bowl-shaped dip in the ground

The K-Pg Boundary

Scientists know about mass extinctions because of rocks and **fossils**. The end of the dinosaurs is marked by a layer of rock. Below this layer there are a lot of dinosaur fossils. Above the layer there are none. This is called the Cretaceous-Paleogene, or K-Pg, boundary.

▼ *These workers are scraping away layers of rock to reveal many dinosaur bones at Dinosaur National Monument in the United States.*

Filling the Gaps

Studying fossils can be difficult. Scientists do not often find the fossil of a whole dinosaur. Usually they find scattered bones. Dinosaur experts fit the pieces together like a puzzle. They have to guess about any missing pieces.

Fossils of tiny animals that lived in the sea give us clues about Earth in the time of dinosaurs. From them we know how hot it was in the sea and on land.

▲ *Occasionally experts make an exciting discovery—a whole skeleton preserved in rock.*

 fossils: the remains of animals and plants that died long ago

▲ *Luis Alvarez and his son Walter point out the K-Pg boundary
in a layer of rock.*

The Big Discovery

Luis Alvarez came up with his asteroid theory after
studying rocks. He looked at rocks that formed at
the same time as the dinosaurs died. Alvarez found
some that contained a **mineral** called quartz.

Shocked Rocks

The quartz was filled with cracks. Scientists call this "shocked quartz." The cracks had been caused by a huge explosion. The rocks also contained a substance called iridium. Iridium is very rare. It could only have come from space. An asteroid crash could explain both the shocked quartz and the iridium.

▼ *"Shocked quartz" is filled with breaks and cracks that can only be caused by a huge impact on the rock.*

"Occasionally there is a question that offers an opportunity for a really major discovery."

Walter Alvarez, Luis's son

mineral: a solid natural substance that has a crystal-like shape

Life After the Asteroid

Scientists believe it took the world two million years to recover from the asteroid impact. Gradually, the Sun warmed the Earth again. New plants began to grow. Mammals, **amphibians**, reptiles, and insects spread across the globe.

▼ *Mammals grew bigger and bigger. The huge horned* Brontotherium *was about 15 feet (4.5 meters) long.*

▶ *This is a fossil of the first known bird,* Archaeopteryx. *It lived at the same time as the dinosaurs.*

The Age of Mammals

The huge dinosaurs had been the kings of the planet. When they were gone, mammals took over. Five million years after the dinosaurs disappeared, the first large mammals appeared. There were more birds, too, now that the giant flying reptiles were extinct.

Mammals probably survived the asteroid crash because they were so small. They could burrow underground to stay warm and safe.

amphibians: egg-laying animals that live on land and in water

Disaster Strikes Again

The death of the dinosaurs was not the last big extinction. Nature had more disasters in store. About 70,000 years ago a **supervolcano** erupted in Indonesia. The ash blocked the Sun. The planet was plunged into a winter that lasted ten years.

▲ *Lake Toba in Indonesia lies in the crater of the supervolcano that erupted thousands of years ago.*

Human Extinction?

Even after the ash cloud cleared, temperatures on Earth stayed cold. Humans struggled to survive. Many did not. In the end, there may have been only about 2,000 people left in the whole world. If there had been one more disaster or a terrible disease, humans might have become extinct.

◀ *Soon after the supervolcano erupted, early humans began to move to different parts of the world.*

Disease has often been a threat to humans. In the 1300s, a disease called the Plague killed one-third of all the people in Europe and Asia.

supervolcano: a giant volcano

Woolly Wipeout

Humans survived the supervolcano's super-eruption. They also survived the last **Ice Age**, which ended about 10,000 years ago. Many animals were not so lucky. Woolly mammoths, woolly rhinos, and sabre-tooth tigers all died out about the time of the last Ice Age.

▼ *A few woolly mammoths survived on an island in the Arctic until about 3,700 years ago.*

New Threats

Early humans may have speeded up this extinction. They hunted the animals for food. In Australia, there were giant kangaroos and enormous lizards called *Megalania*. Both animals were hunted to extinction.

Most experts think that the change in Earth's weather killed these large mammals. They fed on grasslands, which disappeared as the world got warmer and trees began to grow instead.

Ice Age: a long period when Earth's climate is very cold

Hunted to Extinction

Humans have always hunted animals. At first, people caught animals for food or to make clothes from their fur. Later, humans hunted for sport. In the past few hundred years, people have caused many animals to become extinct.

▲ *The very last Tasmanian tiger was killed by a farmer in 1936.*

▲ *The dodo could not fly, so it was an easy target for animal and human hunters.*

Dead as a Dodo

Flightless dodo birds lived on the island of Mauritius for two million years. Then people arrived. Within 100 years, they had killed all the dodos. Many other birds have been hunted to extinction. In 1896, hunters killed the last flock of passenger pigeons.

"The extermination [death] of the passenger pigeon meant that mankind was just so much poorer."

US president Theodore Roosevelt

 flightless: birds that live on the ground because they cannot fly

The Future

The Effects of Extinction

Plants and animals in Earth's **ecosystems** depend on each other. If a plant or animal dies out, the animals that rely on it for food or shelter will also die. Animals that eat other animals are important, too. They keep the numbers of certain species down so they don't eat all the food.

▲ *In 1987, there were 1,500 golden toads left.*
Two years later they were extinct.

▲ *More than half the world's forests have now disappeared, most of them in the last 50 years.*

Who Is Earth's Greatest Enemy?

Humans are the greatest threat to life on Earth. For example, we cut down forests and clear land for farming. This destroys the homes of many animals. Some have not been able to survive.

Right now, we are in the middle of a mass extinction of frogs. This is partly caused by human activity, but a deadly disease is also killing off many frogs.

 ecosystems: all the plants and animals in particular areas

A Changing World

Gases released from cars and factories also harm the planet. They cause the whole world to warm up. Eventually this might cause violent storms or turn the land to desert. Climate change is already affecting many animal species.

▶ *It is getting warmer at the North Pole. As the ice melts, animals such as polar bears find it harder to live and hunt there.*

Going, going, gone

Between 20,000 and two million species have become extinct in the past 100 years. The rate of extinction is getting faster, too. More than 17,000 species are **endangered**. How many of these animals will die out in the next 100 years?

> "It is not the strongest of the species that survives, not the most intelligent that survives. It is the one that is most adaptable to change."
>
> Charles Darwin

endangered: at risk of becoming extinct

Learning More

Books

Why Do Animals Become Extinct?
by Bobbie Kalman
(Crabtree Publishing, 2012)

Extinctions of Living Things
by Michael Bright
(Heinemann, 2009)

Evolving Planet
by Erica Kelly and Richard Kissel
(Abrams Books, 2008)

Websites

http://dsc.discovery.com/earth/wide-angle/mass-extinctions-timeline.html
The Discovery Channel: Mass Extinctions.

http://science.nationalgeographic.com/science/prehistoric-world/mass-extinction/
National Geographic: Mass Extinctions.

http://www.arkive.org/
ARKive: Endangered Species.

Glossary

acid rain Rainwater that contains harmful chemicals

adapt To develop different features to survive in new conditions

amphibians Egg-laying animals that live on land and in water

asteroid A lump of rock and metal that moves around in space

bacteria Tiny creatures made of a single cell

climate change Changes in the weather over a long time

crater A bowl-shaped dip in the ground

ecosystems All the plants and animals in particular areas

endangered At risk of becoming extinct

extinct When something has completely died out

flightless Birds that live on the ground because they cannot fly

fossils The remains or impressions of animals and plants that died long ago

Ice Age A long period when Earth's climate is very cold

mammals Warm-blooded animals that give birth to live young

mineral A solid natural substance that has a crystal-like shape

Permian A period from about 300 to 250 million years ago

radiation Energy that can be harmful to living things

red giant A star that has burned all the hydrogen in its core and grown much larger in size

reptiles Cold-blooded animals that lay eggs

species A particular type of animal or plant

supervolcano A giant volcano

theories Ideas that have not yet been proven true

Index

Entries in **bold** refer to pictures